Into the Next Millennium

Sports

Deborah Cannarella
Jane Fournier

The Rourke Press
Vero Beach, Florida

Photo credits

All photos © copyright: Agence Vandystadt, p. 23 bottom; Allsport, p. 18 bottom (both), 24 bottom (Gray Mortimore), 29 top (Mike Powell); Bombardier, Inc., p. 31 (All rights reserved); Brunswick, pp. 26–27 and 28 bottom; Corbis, p. 13 bottom, 20 top (Historical Picture Archive); 21 top (Charles Harris, Pittsburgh Courier); 22 top (Steve Raymer), 27 top and 30 top (Karl Weatherly); Corbis-Bettmann, pp. 10, 17 top, 19 bottom; Culver Pictures, Inc., p. 11 bottom; The Hockey Hall of Fame, p. 20 bottom; Howard Allen/Allen Studio, p. 19 top; Latrobe Area Historical Society, p. 18 top; Mary Evans Picture Library, pp. 8 bottom, 9 top and bottom, 10 top, 11 top; no credit, p. 21 bottom; Mike Hawley, p. 30 bottom (MIT); The National Art Museum of Sports, p. 14 top (A. B. Frost); North Wind Picture Archives, pp. 6 top and bottom, 4–5 and 7 top, 7 bottom, 8 top, 12 bottom, 4 top and 13 top, 14 bottom (both), 16 top; PhotoDisc, pp. 1 and 24 top, 23 top, 25 both, 27 bottom and 28 top; Princeton University, Seeley G. Mudd Library, Princeton, N.J., p. 15 bottom (Historical Photograph Collection); Stock Montage, Inc., pp. 12 top, 15 top; The Viesti Collection, pp. 4 middle and 16 bottom (Morgan Williams), 4 bottom and 22 bottom (Bavaria); The Vivid Group, p. 29 bottom; Yale University Library Manuscripts & Archives, p. 17 bottom. All cover and introduction page images PhotoDisc.

An Editorial Directions Book
Book design and production by Criscola Design

Library of Congress Cataloging-in-Publication Data

Cannarella, Deborah.
        Sports / Deborah Cannarella, Jane Fournier.
        p. cm. — (Into the next millennium)
        Includes index.
        Summary : Surveys the history of sports and games from first Olympic games up to the present day and speculates on future of sports in the twenty-first century.
        ISBN 1-57103-275-4
        1. Sports—History Juvenile literature. [1. Sports—History.] I. Fournier, Jane, 1955– . II. Title. III. Series.
        GV571.C37 1999
        796'.09—dc21   99-31161
                                                                          CIP

Introduction

The history of the human race is a story of great discoveries and amazing achievements. Since ancient times, people have found creative solutions to problems, met impossible challenges, and turned visions into reality. Each of these remarkable people—and each of their contributions—changed the world they lived in forever. Together, they created the world we know and live in today.

The six books in this series—*Medicine, Transportation, Communication, Exploration, Engineering,* and *Sports*—present a timeline of the great discoveries and inventions that have shaped our world. As you travel from ancient to modern times, you will discover the many ways in which people have worked to heal sickness, shape materials, share information, explore strange places, and achieve new goals. Although they worked with many different tools, their goal was always the same: to improve our quality of life.

As we enter the twenty-first century, we will continue to build on what each generation of people before us has created and discovered. With the knowledge they have given us, we will discover new ways to build, heal, communicate, discover, and achieve. We will continue to change the world in ways we can only begin to imagine.

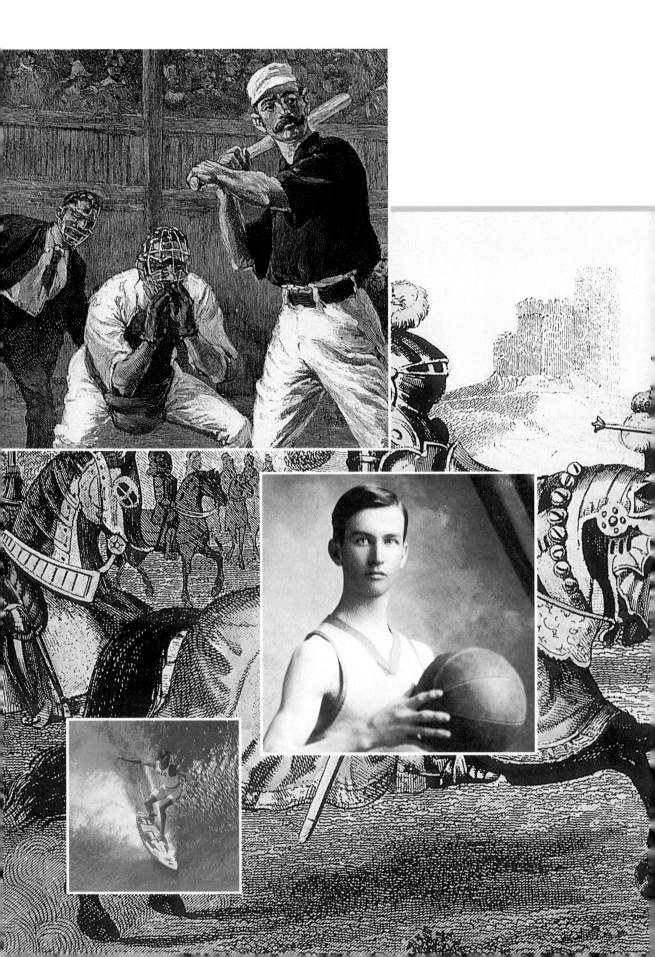

From the *Past*...

776 B.C.

The **Olympic Games,** first held in Olympia, Greece, were day-long contests. At first, the only event was a footrace, called a stade. The athletes ran a distance of about 210 yards (192 m)— the length of the track. Later, events such as the discus throw, the javelin throw, broad jump, chariot racing, and boxing were added. The games were held every four years until A.D. 393.

According to legends, Swiss archer William Tell was forced to shoot an apple off his son's head with a bow and arrow. The folk hero Robin Hood was able to split one arrow with another.

300

By the fourth century A.D., the Romans held public games to celebrate more than 150 holidays. Among their most popular events were **horse racing** and **chariot racing.** These races took place in the hippodrome and the Circus Maximus—two large sports arenas.

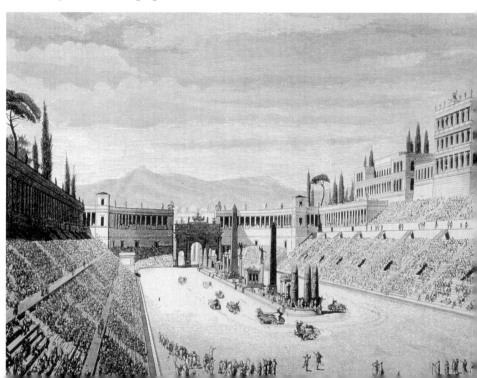

1250

During the thirteenth century, people held mock battles called **jousts.** Two riders on horseback rode toward each other, trying to knock each other onto the ground with long, blunt poles called lances. Another form of jousting is called "tilting the rings." While the horse is galloping, the rider tries to insert a lance through small metal rings.

The Circus Maximus was one of the largest sports arenas ever built. This Roman structure was U shaped and could seat about 250,000 people.

1483

Archery is the sport of shooting a bow and arrow. During the Hundred Years' War (1357–1453), the English mastered a type of bow called a longbow. This bow was 6 feet (1.8 m) long. Tales of their skill in hunting, fighting, and sport were told in songs called ballads. The oldest existing archery club, which is in Scotland, was formed in 1483.

1400

Early peoples first traveled over ice on **skates** made from the bones of elk, reindeer, and other animals. Steel blades, first used in about 1400, made the skates lighter and the skating easier. The first skating club was formed in Edinburgh, Scotland, in 1742.

Football games were played in China as early as 206 B.C. Early footballs had many shapes, from round to oval. Some were made of animal hide and stuffed with feathers or hair. Some were even made from animal bladders that were filled with air.

1432

Since ancient times, people have played many different types of **football.** During the Middle Ages, people played a type of folk football called mêlée, or mellay. This wild game had no rules. Teams of up to 100 players from two different villages played against each other.

1457

Although it resembles a game played by the Romans, the game of **golf** began in Scotland. King James II wrote about the sport in 1457. Early golfers used a leather ball, called a feathery, which was stuffed with feathers. Mary, Queen of Scots (left), who ruled during the mid-sixteenth century, was the first woman golfer.

One version of billiards is played with a small ball and special clubs. This game, which is called golf, resembles the outdoor game that has the same name.

1460

Billiards is played on a table with small balls and a long stick called a cue. There are several versions of the game—including snooker and pocket billiards, also known as pool. Most of the tables have six pockets, into which the players shoot the balls. Early billiard balls were made of ivory. Today, they are plastic. No one knows when billiards began, but the game was first written about in the fifteenth century.

1540

Early **fencing** involved heavy swords, shields, and some wrestling. By the sixteenth century, fencing had become a sport of speed and skill rather than force. A lightweight, blunt sword allowed for quick, controlled movements. In about 1540, King Henry VIII arranged for Italian fencing masters to teach throughout England.

There are three types of fencing swords—epées, foils, and sabers. For protection, fencers wear masks with wire mesh, thick bibs, and canvas or nylon jackets and knickers. They also wear a padded glove on the hand that holds the sword.

1600

The game of **lacrosse** developed from baggataway, a game played by native peoples of Canada. Hundreds of players caught, carried, and threw the ball down a playing field with long wooden rackets. The goals were sometimes miles apart. A game might last three days. French settlers, who began to arrive in Canada in the seventeenth century, named the native game lacrosse. To them, the racket resembled the staff of a shepherd or bishop—which in French is called *la crosse.*

1660

One of the early forms of bowling was a game called **skittles.** Players rolled a wooden or rubber ball toward nine standing pins, which were arranged in the shape of a diamond. The player who knocked down all the pins with the fewest throws won the game. People in the Netherlands played a similar game, called Dutch pins. The bowler could also win this game by knocking over only the middle pin— which was called the kingpin.

Lacrosse was adopted as Canada's national game when the Dominion of Canada was formed in 1867. The game was brought to the United States in 1868.

1719

In 1719, English athlete James Figg opened a **boxing** school in London to teach his style of bare-fist fighting, which included wrestling. In 1743, Jack Broughton introduced the first rules of boxing, which made the sport less dangerous. According to one rule, if a player was knocked down and did not get up within 30 seconds, the game was over. Boxing gloves were not used until the end of the nineteenth century.

1750

In a **steeplechase,** horses and their riders jump over fences, ditches, and other obstacles. According to legend, the race got its name in 1750 when two riders decided to race to a church steeple. The world's most famous steeplechase horse race is the Grand National, which is held near Liverpool, England. The first Grand National race was in 1839.

The rules for the game of soccer were made in 1848. In England and many other countries, soccer is also known as football.

1823

In the early nineteenth century, English students played a type of soccer. During a game at the Rugby School, William Webb Ellis broke the rules by picking up the ball and running. His mistake became a tactic in a popular new game known as **rugby.** Unlike soccer players, rugby players can carry and throw the ball and tackle each other during play. American football is a combination of rugby and soccer.

1839

Some people believe that **baseball** was invented by Abner Doubleday in Cooperstown, New York, in 1839. Other people believe that the game is a version of rounders, which was played in England during the seventeenth century. In both games, the players hit the ball with a bat and run around bases. In rounders, if a runner off base was hit by a thrown ball (or soaked), the runner was out. In baseball, runners off base can be soaked or tagged out.

A footrace run over obstacles is also known as a steeplechase. This sport began as a cross-country race in 1850. It was first included as an Olympic track event in the Olympic Games of 1900.

1841

The Dutch brought their game of Dutch pins to the New World. In one version of the game, the player rolls a large ball, which has a thumbhole, on a plank toward nine pins. By the 1830s, ninepin bowling had become very popular, and people were betting on the game. In 1841, Connecticut and other states banned ninepins. The bowlers simply added another pin—which was how **tenpin bowling** began.

1848

In 1848, E. W. Bushnell made the first all-metal ice skates—strong, lightweight blades that clipped onto a skater's boots. Ice skating soon became popular. Skating clubs opened throughout the United States. A ballet dancer named Jackson Haines added dance movements to skating, which led to a new sport called **figure skating.** Figure skating was an event in the 1908 Olympic Games.

The first roller skates were invented by Joseph Merlin of Belgium in 1760. To show off his new invention, he rode the skates into an elegant party while playing the violin. He had not designed a way to stop or turn, however—and soon crashed into his host's giant mirror!

1851

A yacht is a small, lightweight boat-powered by engine or sail—often used for racing. The word *yacht* is from a Dutch word meaning "ship for chasing." One of the most famous yacht races in the world is the **America's Cup.** The award and the race are named for the schooner *America* (left), which won a race around the Isle of Wight off the coast of England in 1851.

1863

James Plimpton's **roller skates,** designed in 1863, were boots fitted with four, small wooden wheels on springs. Unlike earlier designs, Plimpton's skates could travel in smooth curves. His skates quickly became popular. Indoor roller-skating rinks became active social centers. New sports, such as roller polo and hockey, roller racing, and roller dancing, soon appeared. The first world competitions in roller-skating events were held in 1937.

Modern American football was created in 1874. McGill University and Harvard University played two games. The first was Harvard's kicking game, which resembled soccer. The second was McGill's rugby, which included running with the ball and tackling. Harvard later combined the two playing styles and introduced the new game to other colleges.

The "TASKER" SKATING SHOE.

Sent to any part of the United States

For $3.00

Manufactured by

H. & F. H. TASKER

991 and 993 Fulton Street,

Near St. James Place,

BROOKLYN, N. Y.

1869

The first **college football** game was played between Princeton University and Rutgers College in New Jersey. This kicking game was more like soccer than the modern game of American football, which developed soon afterward. There were 25 players on each team, instead of the 11 players in today's football.

1873

The earliest type of tennis was a game played in France. The players hit a ball over a net with the palms of their hands. In 1873, Major Walter Clopton Wingfield of Wales created equipment and rules for a game similar to the game played today—although his court was in the shape of an hourglass. Wingfield's sport was later called **lawn tennis** and was played with strung rackets on a grass, rectangular court.

Summer Out-Door Games and Toys.

LAWN TENNIS.

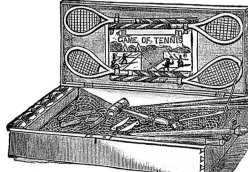

Until within the past few months, this Game was imported entirely, but now we are manufacturing sets in this country in such quantity, that we are able to sell for **$10.00** a complete set that equals, if not excels, such as last year were sold for **$18** to **$20.**

Special Offer for 30 Days Only.

In order to introduce our American Sets into every City, Town, and Village in the United States, we offer, if ordered at once, the regular $10.00 Set, which is complete, for $9.00. Expressage to be paid by the recipient.

This set is handsomely gotten up and will last for years.—Remember, orders must be sent in at once.

ORANGE JUDD COMPANY, 245 Broadway, New York.

In badminton, players hit a cone-shaped object called a shuttlecock over a net with rackets. The game is usually played outdoors on the lawn. The sport got its name from Badminton, an estate in England where it was played 1873. It is a version of a game from India known as poona.

1891

James Naismith, a physical-education teacher at a school in Springfield, Massachusetts, invented the game of **basketball.** As goals, he used two peach baskets—which is how the sport got its name. In 1896, the first college basketball game was played at the University of Iowa. Basketball was included as an event in the 1936 Olympic Games.

People in some ancient cultures lifted rocks—called manhood stones—to prove their strength. In modern **weight lifting,** athletes show their strength by lifting barbells. A barbell is a steel bar with disks of iron or steel attached at each end. The weight may range from 119 pounds (54 kg) to more than 238 pounds (103 kg). An international weight-lifting contest was held in London, England, in 1891.

Table tennis, or ping-pong, is a type of small-scale, indoor tennis game. The players use paddles to hit a hollow ball over a net that is attached to a table. The game developed in England in the late nineteenth century. The first worldwide table-tennis championships were in London in 1927.

1893

Ice hockey is played with two teams of six players on a field of ice. British soldiers first played in Canada in 1855. The first U.S. game was played at Yale University in New Haven, Connecticut, in 1893. Ice hockey may be a version of a game played with sticks and a square wooden block by the native peoples of Canada. In 1894, a Montreal team won the first Stanley Cup—a silver bowl awarded to the champion team of the year.

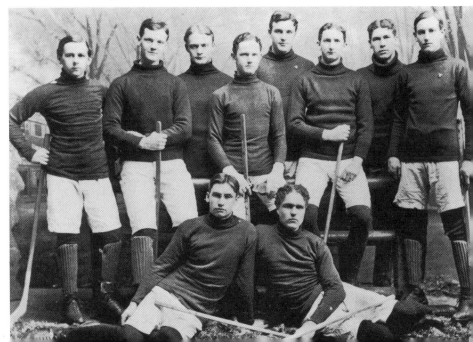

1895

The first **professional football** game took place in Latrobe, Pennsylvania. The team from Latrobe beat the team from the town of Jeannette, with a score of 12–0. The American Professional Football Association, an organization of professional players, formed in 1920. In 1922, the name of the organization was changed to the National Football League (NFL).

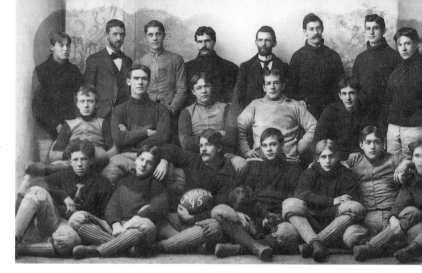

The U.S. Open Championship, one of the world's major golf tournaments, was first held in 1895. This tournament, now held every year, is called an "open" because both amateur and professional golfers participate.

1896

The **Olympic Games**—which had been banned by a Roman emperor in the year 393—were finally held again in Athens, Greece, in 1896. The 43 events included swimming, gymnastics, weight lifting, fencing, and wrestling. Track-and-field events were held in a stadium that had been built in 330 B.C. American runners won 9 of the 12 events. The games lasted for 10 days.

1900

The training and riding of horses is called **horsemanship.** Jumping contests were first included in the modern Olympic Games in 1900. Today's Olympic Games include three contests in the riding and handling of horses. These are called the equestrian events.

One of the main events of the first modern Olympic Games was a marathon—a race of 26 miles, 385 yards (42,186 m). It was held in honor of a Greek soldier who ran from Marathon to Athens, Greece, in 490 B.C., bringing news of a Greek victory in battle.

1903

In 1903, Henri Desgrange organized a bicycle road race. The **Tour de France** has been held every year ever since. More than 100 bicyclists ride about 2,400 miles (4,000 km) through Europe. The race lasts almost one month and ends in Paris, France.

1924

For thousands of years, people have used **skis** to travel over snow and ice. In 1860, Sondre Norheim invented bindings that held the skier's feet securely in the skis. New techniques for stopping and turning developed, and skiing became a popular sport. Contests in cross-country skiing and jumping were included in the first Winter Olympic Games. These contests are known as the Nordic events.

Babe Didrikson Zaharias was one of the greatest women athletes of all time. In 1932, she won three Olympic medals for track and field. She was a member of the women's All-America basketball team and won the U.S. Women's Open golf tournament three times.

The **National Hockey League** (NHL) was organized in Canada in 1917. The first U.S. team in the NHL was the Boston Bruins, which joined in 1924. Every year, the NHL awards a trophy known as the Stanley Cup to the winner of the world's professional ice-hockey championships.

1933

Each July, baseball fans vote for their favorite players to play each other in an **All-Star Game.** Babe Ruth and Lou Gehrig played in the first All-Star Game in 1933. Almost 50,000 fans filled the stands of Comisky Park in Chicago, Illinois, to watch.

In 1875, Captain Matthew Webb became the first person to swim the English Channel. He swam 38 miles (61 km) from England to France in 21 hours 45 minutes. In 1926, Gertrude Ederle became the first woman to swim the Channel, setting a new world record of 14 hours 39 minutes.

Thirteen countries competed in the first international soccer tournament in 1930. Uruguay won a gold trophy, later called the World Cup. The World Cup championships are held every four years.

Alpine ski events were first included in the Winter Olympic Games in 1936. These contests include downhill and slalom racing.

1957

In the track-and-field event known as **pole vaulting,** athletes use long poles to leap over bars set at different heights. Early vaulters used heavy, wooden poles. In 1957, two athletes—Bob Gutowski and Don Bragg—broke world pole-vaulting records with aluminum and steel poles. In 1961, George Davies set a new world record with a fiberglass pole. Today's lightweight poles are made of carbon and fiberglass.

1961

In 1961, Pierre Lemoigne designed a round parachute to attach to the back of a car. As the car moved forward, a person wearing the parachute would rise into the sky. These parachutes were used to train skydivers, who jump from airplanes. A company in Connecticut began to make and sell Lemoigne's parachute, which was called a Parasail. People soon began attaching the parachutes to motorboats, creating a new sport known as **parasailing.**

In 1777, Captain James Cook and his team of explorers watched people riding boards for sport in the ocean waters of Tahiti and Oahu, Hawaii.

1964

Early surfers in Hawaii and Australia rode the ocean waves on wooden boards up to 18 feet (5.5 m) long. Modern **surfboards,** which were first developed in California, are made of strong, molded plastic covered with fiberglass. In 1964, Midget Farrelly won the first world surfboard-riding championships in Manly, Australia, riding the lightweight, California-style board.

1965

The First National Skateboard Championships were held in Anaheim, California, in 1965. Some of the **skateboarding** moves in the freestyle and slalom events were 360s, Handstands, and Nose and Tail Wheelies and Heelies. In the late 1970s, Alan Gelfand invented a new move-popping the board with one foot to make it "fly"—which became known as the "ollie."

In 1972, swimmer Mark Spitz won seven gold medals in one Olympic Game—more than any other athlete in Olympic history. He broke world records in each of the seven events.

In 1961, baseball great Roger Maris hit 61 home runs in one season, setting a new world record. In 1998, his record was broken when Mark McGwire of the St. Louis Cardinals hit 70 home runs. That year, Sammy Sosa also broke Maris's record. He hit 66 home runs for the Chicago Cubs.

In 1963, eighth-grader Tom Sims decided to try out his skateboard on the snow. He called his new board the "Flying Yellow Banana." On Christmas Day 1965, Sherman Poppen attached two skis together to make a **snowboard** for his daughter. His board was called a Snurfer (snow surfer). A year later, the Brunswick Company began to manufacture the Snurfer. Sims's company began to make snowboards in 1977.

1979

In 1976, bicycle racers Gary Fisher and Charles Kelly of California decided to get out of city traffic. They organized downhill bike races along a dirt track about 3 miles (4.8 km) long, with a drop of more than 1,600 feet (488 m). The riders rode "clunkers," old bikes with fat tires. In 1979, Fisher and Kelly began building "off-road" bikes. They called their company Mountain Bikes—which gave the new sport of **mountain biking** its name.

Some people believe that the "extreme" sport of bungee jumping is a form of land diving—an ancient ritual in the South Seas, where people tie vines around their ankles and dive from high towers. In 1997, stuntman Jochen Schweizer set a world record by bungee-jumping out of a helicopter from 8,197 feet (2,500 m).

1984

Rhythmic gymnastics features small equipment, such as ropes, hoops, balls, and long ribbons. Routines are performed to music and include jumps, leaps, and feats of balance and flexibility. Rhythmic gymnastics, which became a sport in 1962, includes individual and group events. Individual events were included in the 1984 Olympic Games. The 1996 Olympics were the first to include group events.

1991

The **women's soccer** team was the first U.S. team to win a world soccer championship. In 1991, the United States beat Norway in the first Women's World Cup, held in China. The mission of the third Women's World Cup, held in 1999, was to "inspire the next generation of female athletes."

1998

In the sport of **skydiving,** a person jumps out of an airplane, free-falls through the sky, opens a parachute, and sails to the ground. Divers jump from as high as 15,000 feet (4,600 m) and open their parachutes when they are about 2,000 to 3,000 feet (600 to 900 m) from the ground. Some skydivers jump as a group, holding their positions to form patterns as they fall. In 1998, a group of 246 skydivers held a pattern position for 7.3 seconds— setting a new world record.

...Into the **Future**

Swifter swimmers.

A new type of swimsuit will help swimmers swim faster. The suits will have tiny fins that will allow the water to flow smoothly across the swimmer's body. They are called hydrodynamic suits—which means that they make the best use of the natural properties of water and objects moving in water. They are being designed by aeronautical engineers (airplane designers).

High-tech alleys.

Bowling alleys will soon be controlled by computer networks. A central computer at the front desk will activate the lanes and compute the fees for playing. As the bowler plays, digital cameras will photograph the pins on the lane. Using the information in the photo, the computer will clear the pins the bowler has knocked down and leave the standing pins in place. The computer will also keep score.

In line and off road.

With new technology, in-line skates are being designed for off-road use. Skaters will be able to travel along mountain trails and down snowless ski slopes. The new skates have drum brakes and large, air-filled wheels designed to roll over rough terrain. The strong metal alloy frames will withstand the shocks and bumps of the trip.

The United States Golf Association tests new golf balls with special computer systems and software. The balls are shot through an indoor passageway. A computer analyzes each ball's speed, spin, and angle—as well as the temperature of the air and wind speed on the virtual (computer-created) golf course.

Virtual sports.

Teams of several players will soon compete in games such as soccer and football without needing a real playing field. In virtual team sports, players stand in front of video cameras. The virtual field is projected onto a screen. As the players move, their movements are recorded by the cameras. Their actions are then translated into scenes of running and ball plays that appear on the screen.

Super shock absorbers.

New technology has led to the development of an improved type of shock absorber. Shocks, bumps, and vibrations are translated into electricity and heat. These new devices can reduce the amount of vibration felt by skiers and bicyclists as they speed over snow and ground. Batters will be able to hit baseballs harder without feeling more sting from the bat.

Bio packs.

Scientists hope that new technology will help reduce the number of injuries and deaths that occur in mountain climbing and other extreme sports. In one experiment, bio packs—a type of body monitor—were attached to climbers of Mount Everest, the highest mountain on Earth. Monitors measured each climber's heart rate, amount of blood oxygen, skin temperature, and body temperature. The information was sent back to doctors at the base camp. The climbers were also equipped with Global Positioning Systems (GPS) so that help could be sent to them if needed.

Better boats.
With new technologies, powered boats for lake and ocean sports—including cruising, fishing, and water skiing—will be sleeker, faster, more comfortable, and less polluting. New types of engines will be designed to produce less noise. With fuel-injection systems and more efficient hull designs, the boats will also burn less fuel—which means they will send less exhaust into the air.

Sports fans will be able to create their own all-star games on computer. With virtual game organizers, sports lovers will be able schedule a match between any two teams—or create teams with any combination of players. The games are never actually played, of course. The computer draws information from a database of statistics to calculate who wins and who loses.

Index

For further reading

Books

Blacklock, Ryan. *Nudes and Nikes: Champions and Legends of the First Olympics.* True Stories series. London: Allen and Unwin, 1997.

Ritter, Laurence R., and Ted Williams. *The Story of Baseball.* New York: William Morrow and Company, 1999.

Smith, Nigel. Illustrations by James Field. *Sports.* Then and Now series. Brookfield, Conn.: Copper Beech Books, 1996.

Web sites

ESPN

The website for the sports network
http://espn.go.com

Hooptown USA

The official site for the Basketball Hall of Fame
http://www.hooptown.com

National Football League

To access information about the NFL
http://www.nfl.com